Contents

Any words appearing in the text in bold, **like this**, are explained in the Glossary.

The big challenge

People travel more and more. A hundred years ago, few people owned a car and aeroplanes had only just been invented. Today, in Europe, North America, Japan, and Australia, many people drive almost everywhere – to work or to school, to supermarkets and shopping centres. Aeroplanes criss-cross the skies. Many people think nothing of flying thousands of miles just for a weekend, while others fly to cities that are only a few hundred miles away. Travelling is convenient and sometimes necessary, but the way we do it is causing problems, not just for us but for the whole world.

Travel backlash

Many cities are choked with traffic. Exhaust fumes from cars, lorries, and buses pollute the air. Inside and outside cities huge swathes of land are taken over by multi-lane highways. As more people use aeroplanes more airports are built, so that today almost every major city has its own airport. Large airports get bigger, taking over even more land, while people who live nearby suffer from the continual noise of planes taking off and landing.

The exhaust gases from heavy traffic pollute the air and add to global warming.

Running out of oil

Cars, aeroplanes, ships, buses, and many trains all rely on oil to power their engines. Oil is separated into different kinds of fuels for different kinds of transport. For example, cars run on petrol and aeroplanes run on **kerosene**, both of which come from oil.

ECO-ACTION

Travel
of the Future

Angela Royston

www.heinemann.co.uk/library
Visit our website to find out more information about **Heinemann Library** books.

To order:
☎ Phone 44 (0) 1865 888066
🖶 Send a fax to 44 (0) 1865 314091
💻 Visit the Heinemann Bookshop at **www.heinemann.co.uk/library** to browse our catalogue and order online.

First published in Great Britain by Heinemann Library, Halley Court, Jordan Hill, Oxford OX2 8EJ, part of Pearson Education.
Heinemann is a registered trademark of Pearson Education Ltd.

© Pearson Education Ltd 2008
First published in paperback in 2009
The moral right of the proprietor has been asserted.

Editorial: Catherine Veitch and Melanie Waldron
Design: Philippa Jenkins and Michelle Lisseter
Illustrations: Bridge Creative Services p.8; Nicholas Beresford-Davies p.10; Philippa Jenkins p.9; Gary Slater pp.11, 14, 23
Picture Research: Melissa Allison
Production: Alison Parsons

Originated by Chroma Graphics (Overseas) Pte. Ltd.
Printed and bound in China by South China Printing Co. Ltd.

ISBN 9780431029870 (hardback)
12 11 10 09 08
10 9 8 7 6 5 4 3 2 1

ISBN 9780431029924 (paperback)
13 12 11 10 09
10 9 8 7 6 5 4 3 2 1

British Library Cataloguing in Publication Data
Royston, Angela
Travel of the future. - (Eco-action)
629'.04

A full catalogue record for this book is available from the British Library.

Acknowledgements
The publishers would like to thank the following for permission to reproduce photographs:
©Alamy pp. **29** (Bryan & Cherry Alexander Photography), **42** (David Hoffman Photo Library), **26** (Doug Webb), **34** (Jeff Greenberg), **16** (Jim West), **22** (Kristin Piljay), **38** (mark wagner aviation-images), **20** (Michael Klinec), **36** (Motoring Picture Library), **18** (Philip Bigg), **19** (Phototake Inc.), **39** (Stock Connection Distribution), **4** (Tom Uhlman), **21** (van hilversum), **23** (vario images GmbH & Co.KG); ©Corbis pp. **5** (David Jay Zimmerman), **12** (Dean Conger), **17** (Ecoscence/Erik Schaffer), **32** (Joel W. Rogers); ©FLPA p. **40** (Nicholas and Sherry Lu Aldridge); ©Getty Images pp. **43** (AFP Photo/Jim Watson), **31** (Digital Vision); ©istockphoto.com p. **37**; ©PA Photos pp. **30**, **15** (AP), **7** (DPA); ©PhotoEdit, Inc. p. **33** (David Young Wolff); ©Photoshot p. **6** (World Pictures); ©SkySails p. **25**; ©Still Pictures pp. **9**, **27** (BIOS Gunther Michel), **13** (C.Garroni Parisi), **28** (David Woodfall), **24** (Friedrich Stark), **41** (Ron Giling), **35** (ullstein – Oed).

Cover photograph of an artist's rendering of a flying solar plane in which Bertrand Piccard, leader of the first hot-air balloon team to circumnavigate the globe without stopover, wants to fly around the world. Reproduced with permission of Corbis/epa.

Every effort has been made to contact copyright holders of any material reproduced in this book. Any omissions will be rectified in subsequent printings if notice is given to the publishers.

During the last hundred years oil has been cheap, but now oil is becoming harder to find and is more expensive. Oil takes millions of years to form (see page 11), and when it runs out there will be no more.

The biggest problem

Traffic jams, noise, pollution, and a growing shortage of oil are important problems, but they are not the biggest issue. The real problem is that burning oil is causing the Earth's **climate** to warm up. This is called **global warming** and the big challenge is, what can be done about it?

Airports need huge areas of space for runways, terminal buildings, and access roads.

Global warming

The way people travel is making the world's climate warmer. During the last hundred years the average temperature at the Earth's surface has risen by 0.8 °C (1.4 °F). This may not sound like much, but a small rise can disrupt the weather and, more importantly, the rate at which the Earth is getting warmer is accelerating. If the Earth continues to heat up as it is now, it will have catastrophic consequences such as more extreme weather, more regions of the world affected by drought, and large areas of coastline flooded by rising seas.

How do scientists know?

Scientists have been concerned about global warming for several decades. They have created computer models that show what might happen as the Earth's temperature rises. These scientists warned the world that action needed to be taken, but many politicians and businessmen did not want to believe them. They argued that the scientists' predictions might be wrong.

It is estimated that 99 percent of the world's glaciers are shrinking.

As Arctic ice disappears, polar bears and many other kinds of animals may become extinct.

But in the last few years something has changed. Instead of scientists relying on computer predictions, they are finding evidence that the effects of global warming have already begun and are often happening faster than they had predicted. They are finding that **glaciers** in the Arctic and Antarctic and on mountain tops have begun to melt, revealing bare land where previously there had been thick ice. Today even politicians accept that global warming is happening.

The effects of global warming

As global warming continues, water from melting glaciers will cause the level of the sea to rise, flooding **low-lying land** near the coast. If global warming continues unchecked, much of New York and London will eventually be below **sea level**, and much of Bangladesh and other low-lying countries will be permanently flooded.

Even before melting ice begins to flood the coast, the world's climates will change. Places that are now farmland may become deserts, while other places will get more rain. Almost everywhere will have more extreme weather. Storms will become more frequent and severe hurricanes will batter the shores of, for example, the southern United States and Queensland in Australia.

DOES IT MATTER?

The climate has been very different in the past. For example, about 12,000 years ago much of northern Europe and North America was covered by ice. The oceans were so much shallower that Alaska was joined to Asia, and Britain was joined to Europe. However, the climate has never changed as fast as it is changing now. It is changing too fast for people simply to adapt to it.

What causes global warming?

Every day a huge amount of energy reaches us from the Sun but most is absorbed by the land and the sea and then released back into the air. Most of this heat passes through the air and escapes into space, but some is trapped in the **atmosphere**. This means that the atmosphere acts like a blanket helping to keep the Earth warm.

Heat traps

Clouds, which consist of **water vapour** and water droplets, absorb some of the heat reflected from the Earth's surface and so do certain gases, including **carbon dioxide**. These gases are called **greenhouse gases**, because they act like the glass in a greenhouse. A greenhouse makes the air inside hotter than the air outside. In the same way, greenhouse gases make the Earth warmer than it would otherwise be. The more carbon dioxide there is in the atmosphere, the warmer the planet gets.

GREENHOUSE GASES

Carbon dioxide, **methane**, **nitrous oxide**, and water vapour are all greenhouse gases. Carbon dioxide and water vapour are by far the most abundant greenhouse gases. Nitrous oxide is more powerful because it traps 300 times as much heat as the same quantity of carbon dioxide, but fortunately there is less of it in the air.

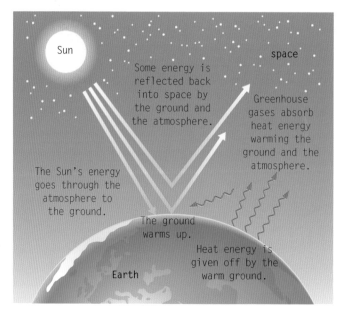

Sun

space

Some energy is reflected back into space by the ground and the atmosphere.

Greenhouse gases absorb heat energy warming the ground and the atmosphere.

The Sun's energy goes through the atmosphere to the ground.

The ground warms up.

Heat energy is given off by the warm ground.

Earth

This shows how the surface of the Earth and the air close to it are heated by greenhouse gases.

Increasing carbon dioxide

The amount of carbon dioxide in the atmosphere has increased rapidly in the last 100 years, particularly in the last 50 years. Carbon dioxide is measured as parts per million by weight (ppm) – that is the number of tonnes of carbon dioxide in, for example, a million tonnes of air. In 1900 it was around 285 ppm. By 2005 this had increased to 381 ppm, which means that there are 381 tonnes of carbon dioxide in every million tonnes of air. The extra carbon dioxide has all been produced by human activities. The oceans and land can only absorb about half of the carbon dioxide being produced now and so the rest builds up in the atmosphere along with the other greenhouse gases.

PLANET VENUS

The surface of Venus is the hottest place in the solar system, apart from the Sun itself. You might expect Mercury to be the hottest because it is closest to the Sun, but Venus's atmosphere is thick with greenhouse gases, particularly methane. During the day the temperature on Venus is about 460°C (860°F).

Heatwaves shrivel plants and can kill people and animals.

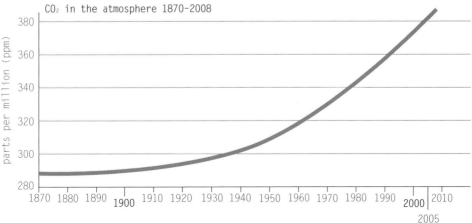

The amount of carbon dioxide in the atmosphere is growing at an increasing rate.

CO₂ in the atmosphere 1870–2008

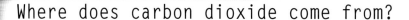

Where does carbon dioxide come from?

Carbon dioxide is produced by all living things. Animals and plants give out carbon dioxide, and when they die and rot or are burned they release more carbon dioxide into the air. However, plants also take in this same carbon dioxide from the air and turn it into food through a process called **photosynthesis**. Animals rely on plants for food, so carbon passes through living things in a continuous circle, called the **carbon cycle**. Living things do not add to the total amount of carbon circulating in the world – it is the burning of **fossil fuels** that does that.

What are fossil fuels?

Fossil fuels are the remains of forests and masses of tiny **marine organisms** that lived millions of years ago. When they died they were buried by **silt** and compressed by accumulating layers of mud. Instead of their carbon being released as carbon dioxide, the remains are very slowly changed into different substances. Plants that grew about 300 million years ago, when the dinosaurs lived, became coal and **natural gas**. Tiny sea creatures that lived up to 400 million years ago formed oil and natural gas.

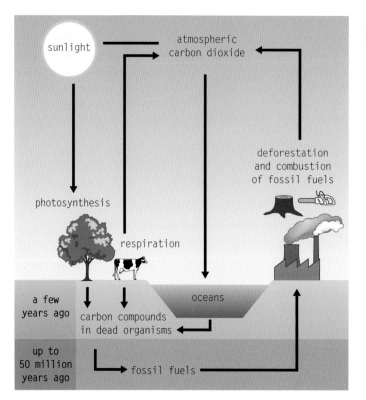

This is the carbon cycle. Carbon dioxide in the air is recycled by plants and living things. Only trees that can live for hundreds of years retain carbon for a long time.

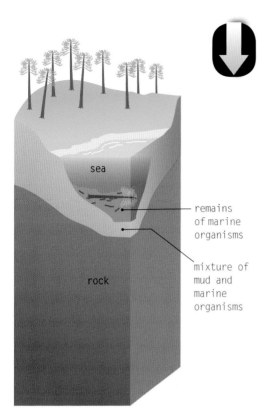

How oil and natural gas were formed.

sea

remains of marine organisms

mixture of mud and marine organisms

rock

The remains of marine organisms collect on the seabed.

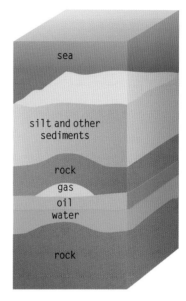

sea

silt and other sediments

rock

gas

oil

water

rock

The pressure of layers of sediment and rock above change marine organisms into oil, gas, and water.

Billions of tonnes of carbon are locked up in fossil fuels. The carbon means that they burn well and make good fuels, but as carbon burns it combines with oxygen to make carbon dioxide, which is released into the air.

Burning fossil fuels

For thousands of years, people burned almost no fossil fuel. They used horses and animals for transport or they walked. Windmills and waterwheels powered their machinery. They burned wood and some coal. Then between 1750 and 1850 engineers invented steam engines that were driven by burning coal. This was called the **Industrial Revolution** and it led to large factories producing many cheap goods. In the 1880s cars were invented that burned oil, and these were followed by the invention of aeroplanes at the beginning of the 20th century. In the last 100 years, people in **developed countries** have come to rely on burning fossil fuels for almost every aspect of their lives.

How does transport contribute to global warming?

Almost all forms of transport burn fossil fuels, mainly oil. In an oil **refinery**, **crude oil** is separated into different substances, including petrol for cars, diesel oil for lorries, buses, trains, and some cars, and kerosene for aircraft. Only bicycles, horses, electric trains, and a few electric cars do not use oil. Trains and cars that use electricity, however, do rely on fossil fuels, since the electricity they use is most likely generated by burning coal, oil, or gas. Electric trains and cars, therefore, still produce carbon dioxide.

Fuel-hungry

Transport is one of the fastest growing users of energy. In 1967 there were fewer than 100 million vehicles in the United States, but today there are more than 237 million. The world now consumes 84 million barrels of oil a day, about 80 percent of which is used for transport. And, of course, burning the oil in those 84 million barrels adds millions of tonnes of carbon dioxide to the atmosphere.

In the United States and the United Kingdom, road vehicles account for about a third of carbon dioxide **emissions**. Although air travel is still one of the lowest users of oil, it is the fastest growing, and a single long-distance flight pumps about as much carbon dioxide into the air per passenger as the average car does in a year. Road and air travel waste the most energy (see page 15) and produce the most carbon dioxide.

Twenty years ago bicycles were the main form of transport on Chinese streets.

Growing demand

So far most of the world's oil has been consumed in developed countries, but this is likely to change. Countries such as China and India are becoming richer and more people there are buying cars and using them for work and for leisure. Burning just a quarter of the current stocks, could make global warming spin out of control.

Avoiding disaster

The good news is that there is still time to avoid the worst catastrophes of global warming. Scientists and engineers are developing new technologies that will allow us to travel without creating carbon dioxide. Some of these technologies are beginning to become available and they will soon become cheaper. Others, such as finding a way of making aeroplane travel **carbon-free**, will take longer.

Today streets in China, like streets in Europe and America, team with motorized vehicles.

Travel of the future

Scientists, engineers, and car designers are gradually making cars less damaging to the planet. They are finding ways of getting more kilometres from each litre of petrol, and they are developing new fuels that are not made from oil. These new technologies will produce vehicles that contribute less and less to global warming. Step by step, they are working towards creating **zero-emission** vehicles – vehicles that emit no carbon dioxide at all.

This is how an internal combustion engine works.

waste gases

intake

piston

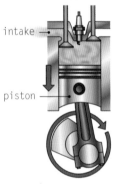   

1 Piston moves down, pulling in a mixture of air and fuel.

2 Piston moves up, compressing fuel mixture. Spark ignites fuel.

3 Mixture burns, pushing piston down.

4 Piston moves up, pushing out unburnt fuel and exhaust gases.

Internal combustion engine

Since cars were invented over a hundred years ago, road vehicles have used the same kind of engine, the **internal combustion engine**, and the same kind of fuel – petrol or diesel oil. In the internal combustion engine, petrol enters each cylinder inside the engine and is ignited. The force of the explosion pushes down the piston in the cylinder. The cylinders fire one after the other and, as each piston is pushed down, they turn a rod, which is connected through other rods and axles to the wheels. The waste gases, including carbon dioxide and unburned fuel, pass out of the engine through the exhaust pipe.

For many years designers have been trying to make the internal combustion engine more efficient. Efficiency measures how much of the energy available in the fuel is actually used to power the vehicle. The internal combustion engine is more efficient than it used to be, but it still wastes most of the energy available in oil (see panel).

Freedom-CAR program

In the early 1990s, California state government in the United States, worried about air pollution and carbon dioxide emissions, required that car manufacturers should develop a zero-emission car, and that by 2003 10 percent of car sales should be for this new type of car. This did not happen and car manufacturers are still trying to achieve a zero-emission car that they can sell at an affordable price. In 2002 President George W. Bush launched the Freedom-CAR program, in which the government and the car companies both invested money to develop zero-emission vehicles. Car manufacturers know that developing such a car will make them money in the future. Scientists know that it will help to save the planet. The race is on!

Many car manufacturers are designing cars that waste as little energy as possible. The body of this car is streamlined and it uses improved fuel and has an improved engine.

New fuels

Biofuels, which are made from crops, trees, and from some animal waste, are an alternative to petrol and diesel oil. The most common biofuel is **ethanol**, a fuel that is similar to petrol and is made by **processing and distilling** crops. Since crops are already part of the carbon cycle (see page 10) turning them into fuel does not add extra carbon dioxide to the atmosphere.

Making ethanol

The best plants for making ethanol are sugar, palm oil, wheat, and corn. The United States, for example, makes ethanol from corn. In some countries ethanol is already mixed with petrol and is used in ordinary car engines. You may not realize it, but the petrol at your local pump probably contains some biofuel. And engines can easily be adapted to burn a higher proportion of ethanol. Brazil has been making ethanol from waste sugar cane since the 1970s and it now accounts for more than half of all the vehicle fuel sold there.

Biofuels for aircraft?

Most aircraft use jet engines, not internal combustion engines, to give them the immense power they need to take off and fly, and they burn kerosene, a fuel made from oil. Some engineers and airline companies are trying to develop a biofuel that will work in aeroplanes.

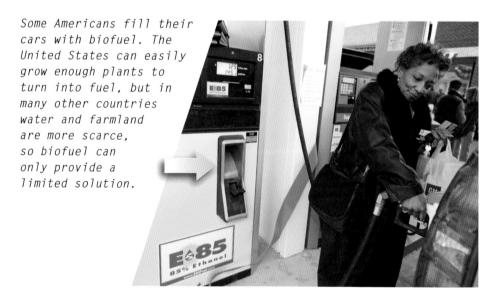

Some Americans fill their cars with biofuel. The United States can easily grow enough plants to turn into fuel, but in many other countries water and farmland are more scarce, so biofuel can only provide a limited solution.

The problem with biofuel

Ethanol might look like an easy solution. Can't we just go on using our cars and flying by aeroplane, but simply use ethanol instead of petrol? The problem is that growing plants for ethanol takes vast amounts of land and huge quantities of water. Most agricultural land is now used to grow food, which we all need and, as global warming progresses, will become increasingly scarce. Instead of using agricultural land, companies are already destroying rainforests from Borneo to Brazil to get land to grow palm oils for biofuel. Not only does this threaten the huge number of species that live there, cutting down the trees releases the carbon that would otherwise have remained stored in them for decades.

Vast plantations
of palm oil are replacing
vital areas of rainforest in Indonesia.

OIL FROM BIOMASS?

Biomass is agricultural waste, such as straw, poultry litter, and cow dung. It is used to produce gas for cooking and for heating homes and larger buildings, such as the space flight centre in Maryland in the United States. However, an American company in Philadelphia called Changing World Technologies is using biomass to produce oil. The oil produced is a mixture of half fuel oil and half petrol. The company claims that the United States could produce enough oil from biomass to replace the oil it currently imports from abroad.

Natural gas

At the moment the world relies on oil for much of its supplies of energy, but soon the age of oil will give way to the age of natural gas. Although natural gas is a fossil fuel, it is less polluting than oil and more effective as a source of energy. The good news is that we have plenty of it, certainly enough to last for a few decades. Natural gas can give us a chance to develop technologies that are carbon-free.

What is natural gas?

Natural gas consists mainly of the gas methane. It is formed in much the same way as oil and coal but it contains very little of the **impurities** that oil contains, such as **benzene** which causes cancer. Methane also has more **hydrogen** and less carbon in each molecule than petrol, so when it is burned it gives off less carbon dioxide. When natural gas is mixed with a small amount of hydrogen, it makes hythane, which produces even less pollution than natural gas. This makes hythane a good fuel for city buses.

*If you visit Brighton, in Sussex, you can hire one of these three-wheeled taxis, which run on **compressed** natural gas. They are called tuk-tuks after similar vehicles, which are popular in Thailand.*

This building is linked to a sewage farm. It collects methane from the sewage to use as fuel for heating.

Natural gas exists in huge volumes below the ground. It used to be burned off at oil wells as a waste gas, but now it is collected and transported in pipelines or in special gas tanker ships to where it is needed. Natural gas is piped into our homes for central heating, hot water, and cooking. Soon we may be filling our vehicles with it too.

Gas-powered vehicles

Gas takes up a lot of space so before it can be used to power a vehicle it has to be compressed. A cylinder of compressed gas takes the place of the petrol tank on board a natural-gas vehicle, often called an **NGV**. These vehicles are already being used. The United States, for example, has more than 80,000 NGVs, including buses, which refuel at compressed natural gas stations throughout the country. Although natural gas is cheaper than petrol, the price of buying an NGV is higher than a conventional vehicle, but as more people become aware of them and buy them their price will fall.

Electric cars

Car manufacturers have spent many years trying to develop cars that run on electric batteries. Electric cars do not pollute the air as they drive along, but they have disadvantages. The batteries have to be recharged often by plugging them into the mains and, if the electricity used to do this is generated in power stations that burn fossil fuels, they add to global warming just like other cars.

How an electric vehicle works

Instead of having a petrol tank and an internal combustion engine, an electric vehicle has an electric motor and a set of batteries. It takes big, heavy batteries to get enough power to drive the vehicle, and the batteries have to be recharged about every 65 to 160 kilometres (40 to 100 miles). Forklifts can be powered by electric motors, as can other vehicles that do not have to travel too far.

Disadvantages

There are three main problems with battery-driven vehicles. The batteries are heavy and bulky. Because a battery is heavy, much of the power it generates is taken up just moving itself. Electric vehicles travel relatively slowly, so they are better suited to driving in towns. In addition, the batteries need to be recharged frequently and usually for several hours or overnight, so they are impractical for long distances.

The battery of this electric car is being recharged. The most modern electric vehicles have increasingly light and efficient batteries

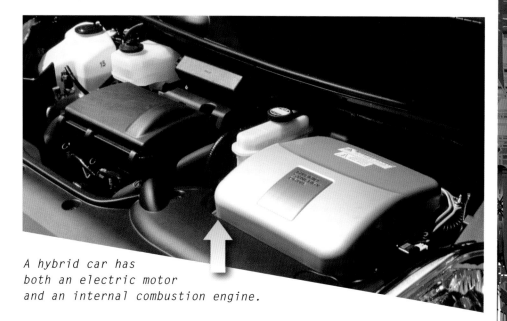

A hybrid car has both an electric motor and an internal combustion engine.

Hybrids

Engineers have found an ingenious way of avoiding the problems of batteries in electric cars. They have developed a **hybrid vehicle** that has both a small internal combustion engine and an electric motor powered by a small battery. The internal combustion engine powers the vehicle when it is being driven gently. When the driver needs more acceleration, the electric motor kicks in, drawing its power from the battery. When the vehicle slows down or brakes, it recharges the battery. Sounds complicated? Happily a computer controls the whole system, so that the driver doesn't have to think about it.

How it works

A hybrid has a small internal combustion engine, so it uses less fuel than a large engine. On its own, a small engine generates less power than a large engine so the car cannot accelerate so fast. The hybrid overcomes this problem by having a second source of power – an electric motor. The electric motor gives the vehicle extra power when it accelerates.

A hybrid avoids the problems of having heavy batteries that often need to be recharged by having a small battery, which is recharged from time to time by the internal combustion engine. Also, when the vehicle brakes or slows down, the electric motor becomes an electric generator. It then generates electricity to recharge the battery. An electric motor uses electricity to produce movement, so it can easily switch to doing the opposite – using movement to generate electricity.

Hybrids in action

Several vehicle manufacturers produce hybrid cars. They are more expensive than conventional cars to buy, but they use less fuel and they will become cheaper. Hybrid engines are particularly useful in towns and cities, where cars are constantly having to stop and start. When drivers have to stop at traffic lights, at least they know that they are recharging the battery!

HYPERCAR

Engineers in Colorado in the United States have used many different ways of getting more power from less fuel in the RMI **Hypercar**. As well as being a hybrid, the body is made of lightweight materials and is totally streamlined, not just to look good but to cut down air resistance all around the car. Everything, especially the tyres, air conditioning, and lights, has been designed to waste as little energy as possible. The result is a car that can do over 40 kilometres to the litre (about 100 miles to the gallon). The inventors of Hypercar are working with different manufacturers to put their ideas into action.

Hybrid engines work well in city buses, which constantly stop and start. Every time the bus stops the battery is recharged.

1617

HYBRID Electric/Alternative Fuel Powered Vehicle

FREE MallRide

This bus uses a hydrogen fuel cell and is already on the streets in Vancouver, Canada; London, and other cities in Europe, the United States, and Australia. However, it is still too expensive to be used generally.

Fuel cells

Scientists are developing a new kind of hybrid electric vehicle that uses a **fuel cell** to supply electricity to the electric motor. A fuel cell uses hydrogen to make electricity and the only waste gas is water. Using hydrogen, the fuel cell is carbon-free and produces energy two or three times more efficiently than any other system. Hydrogen is safer than petrol because it is not poisonous and doesn't harm the environment.

How a fuel cell works

Water consists of two atoms of hydrogen combined with an atom of oxygen. Electricity can be used to split water into hydrogen and oxygen gases in a process called **electrolysis**. Water and electricity can also be made by combining hydrogen and oxygen in a chemical reaction. A fuel cell is like a battery that never needs recharging – provided you keep supplying it with hydrogen, it keeps on generating electricity.

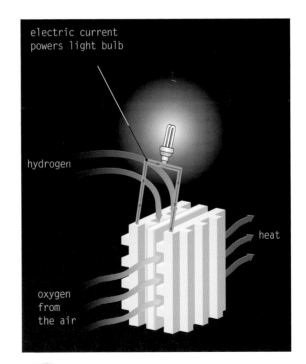

electric current powers light bulb

hydrogen

heat

oxygen from the air

A fuel cell

Gas cylinders
take the place of a petrol
tank in a hydrogen-powered car.

Hydrogen highway

Hydrogen-powered fuel cells could provide us with a carbon-free system for road travel. Buses, lorries, cars, and vans can all be driven using a hydrogen-powered fuel cell to drive an electric motor. However, the technology is too expensive at present and it will be some years before hydrogen vehicles are generally on sale. In the meantime, governments need to set up a system for producing hydrogen fuel and supplying it to filling stations and homes. Some countries are already doing this.

Hydrogen filling stations

In the future, instead of stopping at a petrol station to fill up with petrol, people will probably stop at a hydrogen filling station and fill up with hydrogen. Car manufacturers are working on two main ways of delivering hydrogen. One method is to compress hydrogen into gas cylinders. The other method is to cool hydrogen until it becomes a liquid. Hydrogen, however, has to be cooled to the very low temperature of -253 °C (-423 °F) to make it liquid and then kept at that temperature, so most manufacturers are opting for gas cylinders. Iceland is well placed to set up a hydrogen delivery system and the U.S. state of California is planning hydrogen filling stations along some of its main highways. Norway is already building a hydrogen highway between the cities of Oslo and Stavanger.

A hydrogen future?

If governments start planning and building now, many people could be driving hydrogen vehicles by the year 2040. By then hydrogen fuel cells will be used in many homes for generating some electricity. Eventually hydrogen fuel may be piped to homes and buildings, where it could also be used to fill up cars. When leaving the car in the garage or on the drive at night, the car could be plugged into the home supply and refuelled with hydrogen while its owner sleeps. But we are likely to be using small fuel cells much sooner. By around 2010 they could be used to power laptop computers and mobile phones.

KEEPING IT CARBON-FREE

For hydrogen technology to be carbon-free, the hydrogen cannot be produced from natural gas or by using electricity generated in a power station that burns fossil fuel. This means that governments not only have to re-plan transport, they must also change the way electricity is generated. They have to build new power stations that make electricity from renewable sources, such as water, wind, and sunlight, instead of from fossil fuels, and they have to encourage people to generate their own electricity from **solar panels** and other devices.

Every day inventors are finding new ways to beat global warming. This idea uses a kite and the power of the wind to help pull the ship along.

The technology is already being developed that will help to create a carbon-free world, at least as far as transport is concerned. Low-carbon fuels, biofuels, and hybrid cars that will eventually be powered by hydrogen will lead to zero-emission vehicles. So can people wait for technology to save the world from global warming? The answer unfortunately is no. It will take up to 30 or 40 years before even half the world's transport is carbon-free and the Earth cannot wait that long.

More than a year after Hurricane Katrina devastated New Orleans and surrounding areas in Louisiana, U.S.A., large parts were still uninhabitable.

Present dangers

Global warming is happening now. Glaciers are melting and adding extra water to the oceans. The world is experiencing more extreme weather – more droughts, more hurricanes, more heatwaves, and more flooding – than ever before. Droughts shrivel crops in East Africa, while parts of south-east Spain are as dry as the Sahara. In Europe the hottest summers ever recorded have all occurred since the year 2000 – in August 2003 about 35,000 people died in a heatwave that scorched most of Europe. The hurricane season brings severe storms more often, pounding the coasts of the Caribbean and surrounding countries. In August 2005 Hurricane Katrina flooded and destroyed most of the coastal city of New Orleans in southern United States.

More to come

Even if it were possible to stop burning all fossil fuels now, the Earth will continue to warm up. It takes years for additional carbon dioxide in the atmosphere to contribute to global warming, so some of the carbon dioxide and other greenhouse gases we have already produced have yet to affect the Earth's temperature.

If people do not act now, global warming will accelerate even faster.

The islands of Tuvalu will disappear under rising sea levels.

Tipping points

Global warming is already happening much faster than scientists originally predicted. So far the increase in global temperature is mainly due to people burning fossil fuels and other human pollution. As the temperature increases, however, several natural events beyond people's control will begin to happen that will accelerate global warming. They are called **tipping points** and some could be less than 10 years away.

Arctic ice

As the Earth becomes warmer the ice that covers the Arctic Ocean will begin to melt, revealing the dark water below. At present the white ice reflects most of the Sun's heat back into space. When the ice melts, however, the dark water below will absorb the Sun's heat, raising its temperature and melting more ice.

Sea ice reflects the Sun's heat, helping to keep the Earth cool, but dark open water absorbs heat from the Sun.

Arctic bogs

Around the Arctic Ocean is boggy land that is permanently frozen below the surface. This is called **permafrost**. Locked into the frozen land are vast quantities of methane, produced by the slowly rotting plants in the swamp. As the Earth warms, the permafrost will melt and every year millions more tonnes of carbon dioxide and methane – one of the more powerful of the greenhouse gases – will escape into the air.

Amazon rainforest

The Amazon rainforest covers about 6.4 million square kilometres (2.5 million square miles) but loggers and farmers are destroying vast areas of it. Between 2000 and 2006 150,000 square kilometres (about 58,000 square miles) were cleared, but there is another threat that we cannot control. We usually think of rainforests as being constantly wet, but at certain times of the year some parts, particularly around the edge, become dry. In these drier areas trees already catch fire, burning down many other trees and releasing carbon dioxide. Each year the Amazon rainforest will become smaller and, if nothing is done, it could all eventually be lost.

GOOD (AND BAD) NEWS

Melting sea ice does not add to rising sea levels because, as the ice melts, it shrinks to take up the same space in the ocean as the ice did. And the bad news? As the oceans warm, the seawater expands, pushing up sea levels.

Forests may catch fire when trees are struck by lightning.

Race to save the planet

Scientists calculate that the Earth has only until about 2016 before tipping points begin to push global warming beyond control. The Earth cannot wait for new technology to save it. For example, even though some NGVs and hybrid cars (see pages 19 and 21) are available now, they are still too expensive for many people to buy them. They will become cheaper and more common, but it will probably take many years before they make a real difference. In the meantime people have to act now to reduce the amount of fossil fuel they burn. The good news is that when it comes to travelling, there are many different things people can do to make a difference.

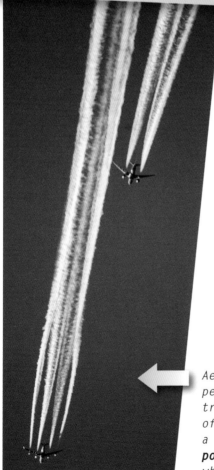

How much do people need to save?

The land and the oceans can absorb about half of the carbon dioxide emitted due to human activities. It is the other half that is causing all the trouble. Emissions from **developing countries** will probably increase, as the standard of living of their people improves. To counteract global warming the developed countries will need to reduce their emissions by up to 80 percent before the end of this century.

*Aeroplanes create more carbon dioxide per kilometre than any other form of transport. They not only leave trails of water vapour in the sky, they emit a stream of carbon dioxide and other **pollutants** high in the atmosphere where they will do the most damage.*

Cutting out waste

Most people are very wasteful in the way they use energy – they could reduce their carbon dioxide emissions by a massive 30 percent just by cutting out waste. The following pages will explain how to do this by changing the way you travel. For example, walking, riding a bike, and taking public transport saves the carbon dioxide that would be emitted travelling by car. It may be a small change, but all the small savings taken together can make a big difference – the difference perhaps between global warming getting out of control and holding it in check until carbon-free energy is available for everyone.

The bigger picture

Nevertheless one person cannot save the planet on their own. One of the most helpful things you can do is to persuade other people to cut out waste too. The biggest polluters are companies and large organizations. They need to cut out waste too and governments need to act together to solve the problems of global warming.

Many car journeys are unnecessary. Taking more care in deciding when to go by car is something everyone can do.

Drive less

It is very easy if you are going a short distance just to jump in a car. It is even easier if you can persuade someone else to drive you! However, with a little bit of planning it is often possible to walk or cycle instead of going by car. It may take a bit longer, but walking and cycling help people keep fit and healthy. People often drive to the local shops, to take their children to school, to see their friends, and to go to the gym or other sporting activities. In Britain most car journeys are less than 3 kilometres (2 miles).

Walking and cycling

Short journeys of 3 kilometres (2 miles) or less should take less than half an hour if you walk fast. If you go to a local school, this is probably within about 1.5 kilometres (about a mile) of where you live, so walking is definitely the best way to get there. You only have to get up a bit earlier to make sure that you are not late. For journeys of up to 5 or 6 kilometres (3 or 4 miles), cycling is a good option. Remember, however, to have your bicycle regularly checked and serviced, to use safe routes, and to wear a safety helmet and brightly coloured, fluorescent clothes.

Cycling to school or to work is a good way to keep fit.

Healthy exercise

Walking and cycling are healthier than driving. They exercise your leg muscles, your heart, and lungs. They help to keep your body fit and your mind alert. When you breathe in you take more oxygen into your blood. Much of the extra oxygen is used by our muscles as they work harder, but the rest of the oxygen helps the brain and other parts of your body to work better.

Walking and cycling not only provide good exercise and help to save the planet, they are cheap too, provided you already have a bicycle. Driving consumes petrol and wears out the engine. Petrol will become more expensive as it becomes more difficult and costly to extract it from the ground.

SAFE ROUTES

Many people drive to places by car because they feel safer that way. When few people cycle or walk, the streets may seem dangerous. The safest way to cycle is along special cycle paths that are separate from the traffic. Many schools are creating safe walking routes to and from school. If your school has a safe route, use it if you can. If it doesn't, talk to your school about creating one.

Walking to school with your friends is fun and safer than walking on your own.

33

By using the bus, each of these people is saving several kilograms of carbon dioxide emissions.

Use buses and trains

If you are going on a longer journey, plan ahead to see if you can use public transport instead of going by car. Many cars have only one or two people in them, so a single bus can replace more than 40 cars. This not only saves carbon dioxide emissions, it creates less congestion too. Trains carry even more people than buses and, if the rail service is good, they are much faster than driving by car.

Buses

If your school is too far away to walk to, you may be able to go by bus, either by school bus or public bus. Most large towns and cities have bus services to take people in and out of the city centre and from one suburb to another. For a local bus service to work well, however, the buses need to run regularly so that people do not have to wait too long. It helps if there are special bus lanes so that buses are not held up in traffic. The better the bus service the more people will use it.

Trains and coaches

Large cities have suburban trains that speed you right into the city centre. Trains usually run to a more regular timetable than buses, so, provided you check the train times in advance, you should not have to wait long. To travel from one city to another you can usually go by train or by coach. It is often more comfortable to travel this way than by car, because you can read, eat, and even walk about.

Car-sharing

Some people have to drive because they live too far from a bus route or train station. If you do have to go somewhere by car, see if you can share your car with other people. Many people car-share to get to and from work. You could link up with students who live near you, and your parents could take it in turns to drive you all to school. If you are meeting friends somewhere, arrange to go in one car instead of all being driven separately.

HOW THEY COMPARE

Driving by car creates about three times the amount of carbon dioxide as travelling by train or bus. For example, you would emit 30 kilograms (66 pounds) of carbon dioxide if you travelled 160 kilometres (100 miles) by car, but only 11.6 kilograms (25.5 pounds) by train and 9 kilograms (19.8 pounds) by bus.

The fastest trains travel at around 320 kilometres an hour (200 miles per hour) - more than twice as fast as a car. And you do not have to find a place to park when you arrive!

Using less petrol

The more petrol a car uses the more carbon dioxide it produces. There are several things you can do to reduce the amount of petrol your family uses. The most important is to cut down the number of journeys you make by car. Get your family to organize things so that they do as many different errands on one journey as possible.

This car looks much like other cars, but it is driven by a hybrid system. It does about 21 kilometres per litre (60 miles per gallon), and newer models will do even better.

HOW TO USE LESS PETROL

These are some things that can reduce the amount of petrol a car uses:

- Drive more slowly and more evenly.
- If you are travelling at less than 65 kilometres per hour (40 miles per hour), open the window instead of using air conditioning.
- Remove the roof-rack when it is not being used – roof-racks make the car less streamlined.
- Unload any heavy things that you don't need to carry – the more weight in the car the more petrol it uses.
- Remind your parents to have the car serviced regularly – clogged air filters increase the amount of petrol used.

SUVs have several features that make them consume more petrol than the average car.

roof-rack reduces streamlining

bars reduce streamlining

four-wheel drive

heavy weight (2 to 4 times heavier than average cars)

Gas-guzzlers

On average, cars with big engines consume more petrol than those with small engines, and **four-wheel drive cars**, such as **SUVs** (sport utility vehicles), consume the most. SUVs use more petrol because they are heavier than a standard car and they are unstreamlined. Streamlining cuts down air resistance, so an unstreamlined SUV has to use more fuel to push through the air.

Old cars usually use more petrol than newer ones. This is because the engine is worn and does not work so well and because the engines of newer cars have been improved so that they get more kilometres (miles) to the litre (gallon).

Hybrids

Hybrid cars are becoming more common and they will become cheaper. If your family is thinking of buying a new car, persuade them to consider buying a hybrid. A hybrid will perform as well as a fast car, but use much less petrol when driving in a town or city.

SHOULD GAS-GUZZLERS BE BANNED?

Some gas-guzzlers do as little as 20 kilometres to the litre (12 miles per gallon), whereas a hybrid can do up to 95 kilometres to the litre (60 or more miles per gallon). A study in Europe suggests that cars that do less than 72 kilometres to the litre (45 miles per gallon) should be made illegal by 2010. Do you agree?

Sixty years ago only a few people could afford to fly. Now flying is often cheaper than going by train.

Fly less

Flying is the fastest-growing form of transport, but it creates the most pollution. Flights have become cheaper and more people are using them. Some flights are necessary but many are a luxury. Many people fly to a city just for a weekend's holiday, and many fly when they could just as easily go by train or bus. People need to think carefully before taking a flight to decide whether it is really necessary.

Pollution trails

Aircraft generate huge amounts of pollution compared to other forms of public transport. An aeroplane flight produces 10 times as much carbon dioxide per passenger as a train does for the same journey. Travelling from Edinburgh to London and back by train, a journey of 1,300 kilometres (about 800 miles) for example, creates 80 kilograms (about 180 pounds) of carbon dioxide for each passenger. Flying from Edinburgh to London and back creates 800 kilograms (about 1,770 pounds) per passenger. A family flying between Florida and London on holiday can make as much carbon dioxide between them as driving their family car for a whole year.

Fuel tax

Why are flights so cheap? One reason is that, although aircraft consume vast amounts of fuel, airlines do not pay tax on aircraft fuel. Some of the price that road vehicles pay for petrol or diesel is in taxes that the government collects. So far no government in the world charges aircraft fuel tax for international flights, because they say it would put their own airlines at a disadvantage compared to those of other countries. Governments would need to agree to charge the same amount of tax.

Video phones

One way of avoiding flying is to use a video phone, which allows you to see the person you are speaking to. And, if you make the call using broadband on your computer, it will not cost you anything. Provided you and the person you are calling have video cameras linked to your computers, you can talk to each other as though you were in the same room. Business people can meet and talk to their clients or colleagues in another country using video conferencing. Each person can see everyone else on television screens.

New technology can make some flights unnecessary. These business people are taking part in a video conference with colleagues in another country. This saves them having to fly to meet in person.

The physic nut plant (Jatropha curcas) is an example of a carbon-offsetting project in the Philippines. Jatropha oil is produced from the seeds and used as biofuel.

Don't be fooled

Some people have come up with an idea called **carbon offsetting**, as a way of "paying" for carbon emissions. The idea is that an individual calculates how much carbon dioxide they are responsible for and then gives money to a company that, for example, plants trees that will absorb that amount of carbon dioxide. This might sound like a good solution, but does it work, or does it just give people an excuse to go on producing the same amount of carbon dioxide as before?

Calculating carbon emissions

There is an Internet site (see page 47) that calculates how much carbon dioxide is produced when a journey is made by car, bus, train, or aeroplane. You can also calculate carbon emissions from other sources, such as your home. This is a useful thing to do as it helps you to see which activities contribute most to global warming.

A carbon-offsetting company converts the amount of carbon dioxide into an amount of money that they promise to spend for you in an activity that will cut carbon dioxide emissions elsewhere. Activities include handing out **long-life light bulbs** and wood stoves, as well as planting trees.

Does carbon offsetting work?

The main problem with carbon offsetting is that you pay for emissions already made by investing in things that will produce savings in the future. Suppose, for example, your family car produces 3 tonnes (3.3 tons) of carbon dioxide a year. The carbon-offsetting company might calculate that all you have to do is pay for 57 trees to be planted. The trees, however, will take up to 100 years to soak up the same amount of carbon dioxide that your car produced in a year. More importantly, if people feel that they can offset carbon dioxide so cheaply and easily, they might be fooled into thinking they do not have to change their behaviour.

Problems of carbon offsetting

Carbon-offsetting companies are in business to make money and they want people to believe their schemes will work. But there is no way of knowing whether the money will actually save the carbon dioxide, even over a long period. No one knows how many of the trees planted will actually grow, or whether the trees that grow will survive for 100 years. One Cambridge scientist has said that telling people to plant trees to reduce global warming is like telling them to drink more water to keep down rising sea levels!

Planting trees and other projects that reduce carbon dioxide emissions are good things to do, but people in developed countries must also cut the amount of carbon dioxide they produce.

Act together

People need to cut carbon dioxide emissions and the more that you and your family do, the better. There is only so much that one person or family can do, however, and you can achieve even more if you persuade others to join you. Organizations, such as schools, offices, shops, and factories, use large amounts of energy. A school, for example, may create about 100 times the amount of carbon dioxide as your home. Think about the local community and whether things can be better organized, and about whether the politicians are doing as much as you think they should to combat global warming.

These people are hoping to persuade their local council to ban cars in this road.

Your school

How does your school organize transport? Does it encourage people to walk to school? Does it discourage people from driving in separate cars? When you go somewhere on a school trip, does the school organize the transport to create the least carbon dioxide?

Local community

Does the local council do as much as they could to encourage walking, cycling, and public transport? Would creating more cycle lanes and bus lanes help? Could they make it more expensive to go by car, for example by charging more for parking and charging to enter the city centre?

Carbon trading

National governments need to work together to agree to reduce carbon dioxide emissions. To prevent the worst effects of global warming the richer countries need to reduce their output of carbon dioxide each year so that by 2050 they have reduced it by 60 or even 80 percent. One scheme that governments are talking about is **carbon trading.** Each country is allocated an amount of carbon dioxide that they are allowed to emit. Countries that produce more can buy credits from countries that produce less than their allowance. In this way developing countries get extra money to help them.

Politicians meet with U.S. President George W. Bush at the White House. Elected politicians are often reluctant to bring in changes they think will be unpopular with voters. Write to a local representative pointing out the dangers of ignoring global warming.

Problems with carbon trading

There are two main problems with carbon trading. The first is whether the allowances for each country will be set low enough to produce the savings required. The second is that, like carbon offsetting (see page 41), it provides an excuse for developed countries to carry on polluting. The only way the world can combat global warming is to work together to change the way people live. People have to change the way they travel and use energy.

43

Glossary

atmosphere mixture of gases that surrounds a planet, such as Earth

benzene very poisonous gas that can cause leukaemia

biofuel fuel for vehicles that is made from plants or other organic material

carbon cycle process through which carbon moves between living things and the atmosphere

carbon dioxide gas that is found mainly in the atmosphere

carbon offsetting balancing the carbon or carbon dioxide you have produced by paying for a reduction in carbon or carbon dioxide elsewhere

carbon trading system whereby companies and/or countries are each allocated a permitted weight of carbon dioxide they can produce. Companies or countries that produce more than their allocation buy extra allowances from companies or countries that produce less than their allocation.

carbon-free without producing carbon or carbon dioxide

climate usual pattern of weather expected at different times of the year

compressed squeezed under pressure to occupy a smaller volume

crude oil unrefined oil

developed country nation, such as the United States or Australia, with a high standard of living due to its advanced economy

developing country nation, such as Kenya or India, where most people rely on farming and are poorer than those in developed nations

electrolysis process of using an electric current to produce a chemical change

emission release of waste substances into the environment, particularly into the atmosphere, rivers, or the sea

ethanol a biofuel

fossil fuel coal, oil, or natural gas. They are called fossil fuels because they formed millions of years ago.

four-wheel drive car car whose engine turns all four wheels of the car. In most cars the engine turns only the back wheels to drive the car.

fuel cell device that produces electricity by combining the gas hydrogen with oxygen

glacier large, slow-moving mass of ice in the Arctic, Antarctic, or on high mountains

global warming increase in the average temperature of the surface of the Earth

greenhouse gases gases in the atmosphere that trap the Sun's heat and so lead to global warming

hybrid vehicle vehicle that uses both a small internal combustion engine and an electric motor to power the vehicle

hydrogen gas that is one of the gases in the atmosphere and which makes a good fuel

Hypercar car designed to use every possible way of reducing fuel consumption

impurities substances that contaminate or pollute something

Industrial Revolution changes in Britain in the 18th and 19th centuries which led to the mass production of goods in large factories

internal combustion engine engine that burns fuel such as petrol or natural gas inside the engine to produce movement

kerosene fuel derived from oil that is used by aircraft engines

long-life light bulb light bulb that lasts longer than traditional bulbs. A compact fluorescent light bulb, for example, lasts eight times as long.

low-lying land land that is not much higher than sea level

marine organisms tiny plants and animals that live or lived in the sea

methane natural gas and one of the greenhouse gases

natural gas fossil fuel produced as a gas in the rocks

NGV natural-gas vehicle. A vehicle that uses natural gas as its fuel.

nitrous oxide a greenhouse gas

permafrost soil or rock below the surface that remains permanently frozen, even though the soil on the surface may melt at warmer times of the year

photosynthesis process in which carbon dioxide from the air and water is combined using chlorophyll and the energy of sunlight to produce sugar. Photosynthesis mostly takes place in the leaves of green plants and produces oxygen as a waste gas.

pollutant something which pollutes or contaminates something

processing and distilling transforming one thing into another by means that include separating out part of a liquid by heating it to different temperatures

refinery building where oil is refined, or separated, into different substances

sea level level of the sea halfway between high and low tides

silt dust or powder that settles to the bottom of a liquid

solar panel device that uses the heat of the Sun to heat water for a building or to generate electricity. Also known as a photovoltaic panel.

SUV sports utility vehicle, the name given to many cars that are mainly designed to be driven off-road over rough land but are usually used to drive on ordinary roads

synthetic materials materials, such as plastic, nylon, and acrylic, that are made from oil

tipping point critical point in a changing situation that triggers further unavoidable changes

water vapour water in the form of a gas

zero-emission without any emission

Some websites, such as *www.hydrogen.co.uk*, give information about specific topics – in this case, the potential and benefits of using hydrogen as a fuel. Other websites give information about many aspects of global warming, its consequences, and what you can do. This is a selection of both kinds of websites:

Global warming

www.bbc.co.uk/climate/
Website produced by the BBC. It explains simply and clearly the greenhouse effect, the impact of global warming, and the adaptations we shall need to make. Go to Adaptation and then Life at Home to see what you can do.

www.epa.gov/climatechange/
Website of the U.S. Environmental Protection Agency, which explains global warming and its effect on the environment and eco systems and suggests various things you can do.

www.ecocentre.org.uk/global-warming. html
Explains the greenhouse effect and where greenhouse gases come from.

climate.wri.org/topic_data_trends.cfm
Gives a world map in which the area of each country is in proportion to the weight of carbon dioxide it emits.

www.energyquest.ca.gov/story/ chapter08.html
Explains how coal, oil, and natural gas were formed.

www.commondreams.org/ headlines06/0312-03.htm
Gives an article published in the *Observer* newspaper about tipping points in the Arctic and how they will accelerate global warming.

www.climatehotmap.org/
A website that gives a map showing early warning signs of global warming in different continents. Produced by several organizations including World Resources Institute, Environmental Defense, and World Wildlife Fund.

www.earthinstitute.columbia.edu/ crosscutting/climate.html
Website of the Earth Institute at Columbia University in the U.S. It outlines the consequences of global warming and suggests some things you can do.

www.greenpeace.org.uk/climate/ climatechange/index.cfm
Website of U.K. environmental campaigning organization, Greenpeace, with facts and predictions concerning global warming.

www.sierraclub.org/globalwarming/qa/
Website covering global warming and things you can do about it.

www.climatecrisis.net/
Website for the film *An Inconvenient Truth*, which includes facts about global warming and things you can do.

www.greener-driving.net
Website produced by the United Nations Environment Programme, which gives tips about motoring.

www.eta.co.uk/pages/Green-Tips/19/ default.htm
More tips on how to save emissions from your car.

SYNTHETIC TREES

Scientist, Klaus Lackner, has designed a synthetic tree that absorbs 1000 times more carbon dioxide than a real tree. The tree would act like a filter, taking carbon dioxide out of the air and storing it underground. Lackner calculates that one synthetic tree could remove 90,000 tonnes (99,000 tons) of carbon dioxide. Only 250,000 trees would be needed worldwide to remove all of the excess carbon dioxide from the air. However, he has yet to build a single tree.

Zero emissions

http://www.ucsusa.org/clean_vehicles/ cars_pickups_suvs/californias-zero-emission-vehicle-zev-program.html
Website charting the history of California's zero-carbon-emission program.

Biofuels

www.shell.com/biofuels/
Website produced by the oil company Shell about different kinds of biofuels.

www.guardian.co.uk/life/feature/ story/0,13026,960689,00.html
An article from the *Guardian* newspaper about using turkey waste to produce oil and gas.

Natural gas fuel

www.fuelingthefuture.org/contents/ NaturalGasVehicles.asp
Tells you all about natural gas vehicles (NGVs).

Electric cars

www.worldchanging.com/ archives/002515.html
Website promoting the increasingly popular electric car G-Wiz made in India.

Hybrids

www.rmi.org/sitepages/pid191.php
Website produced by the Rocky Mountain Institute about the Hypercar and how it works.

Hydrogen fuel

www.hydrogen.co.uk/h2/hydrogen.htm
Gives diagram showing how hydrogen could be produced from renewable sources of electricity and used to power buildings and transport.

www.fctec.com/fctec_types_pem.asp
Tells you about how a hydrogen fuel cell works. The proton exchange membrane fuel cell (PEM) is the best kind of hydrogen fuel cell for buildings.

www.hydrogenhighway.ca.gov/
Gives information and updates about California's hydrogen highway.

Carbon offsetting

www.carbonfootprint.com/calculator.html
Website that allows you to calculate how much carbon your family produces.

Index